ARE YOU READY FOR AN ADVENTURE..?

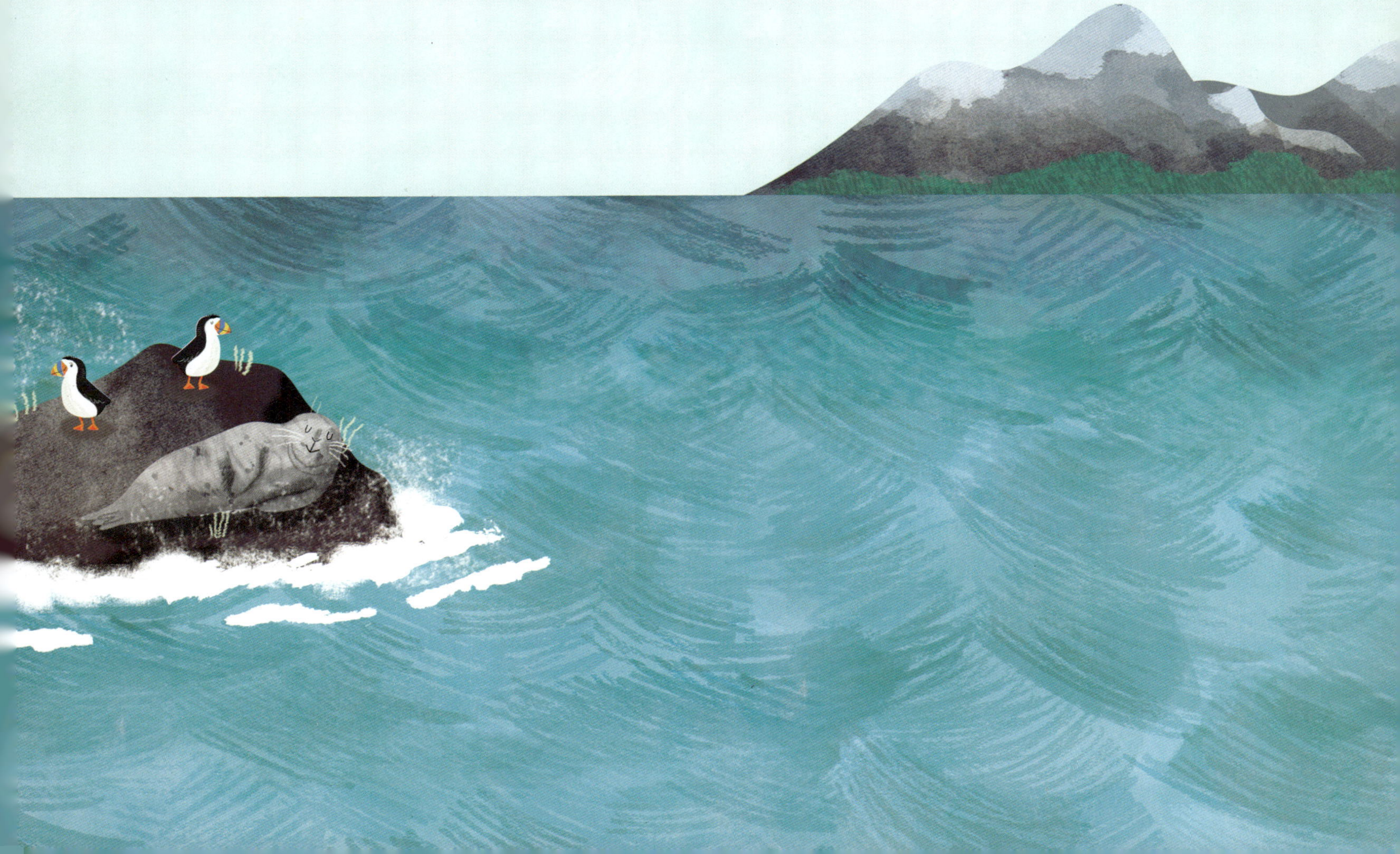

ACKNOWLEDGEMENTS

Publishing Director	Piers Pickard
Publisher	Tim Cook
Commissioning Editor	Jen Feroze
Illustrator	Pippa Curnick
Designer	Andy Mansfield
Print production	Larissa Frost,
	Nigel Longuet

Thanks to: Hayley Warnham, Dr Kim Bryan,
Jennifer Dixon

Published in February 2016 by Lonely Planet Global Limited
ISBN: 978 1 76034 040 7
ABN 36 005 607 983
www.lonelyplanetkids.com
© Lonely Planet 2016
Printed in Malaysia

10 9 8 7 6 5 4 3

Lonely Planet Offices

AUSTRALIA
The Malt Store, Level 3, 551 Swanston St,
Carlton, Victoria 3053 T: 03 8379 8000

IRELAND
Unit E, Digital Court, The Digital Hub,
Rainsford St, Dublin 8

USA
124 Linden St, Oakland, CA 94607
T: 510 250 6400

UK
240 Blackfriars Rd, London SE1 8NW
T: 020 3771 5100

STAY IN TOUCH lonelyplanet.com/contact

MIX
Paper from
responsible sources
FSC™ C021741

Paper in this book is certified against the
Forest Stewardship Council™ standards.
FSC™ promotes environmentally responsible,
socially beneficial and economically viable
management of the world's forests.

lonely planet kids

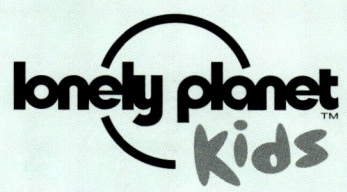

LET'S EXPLORE OCEAN

Pippa Curnick

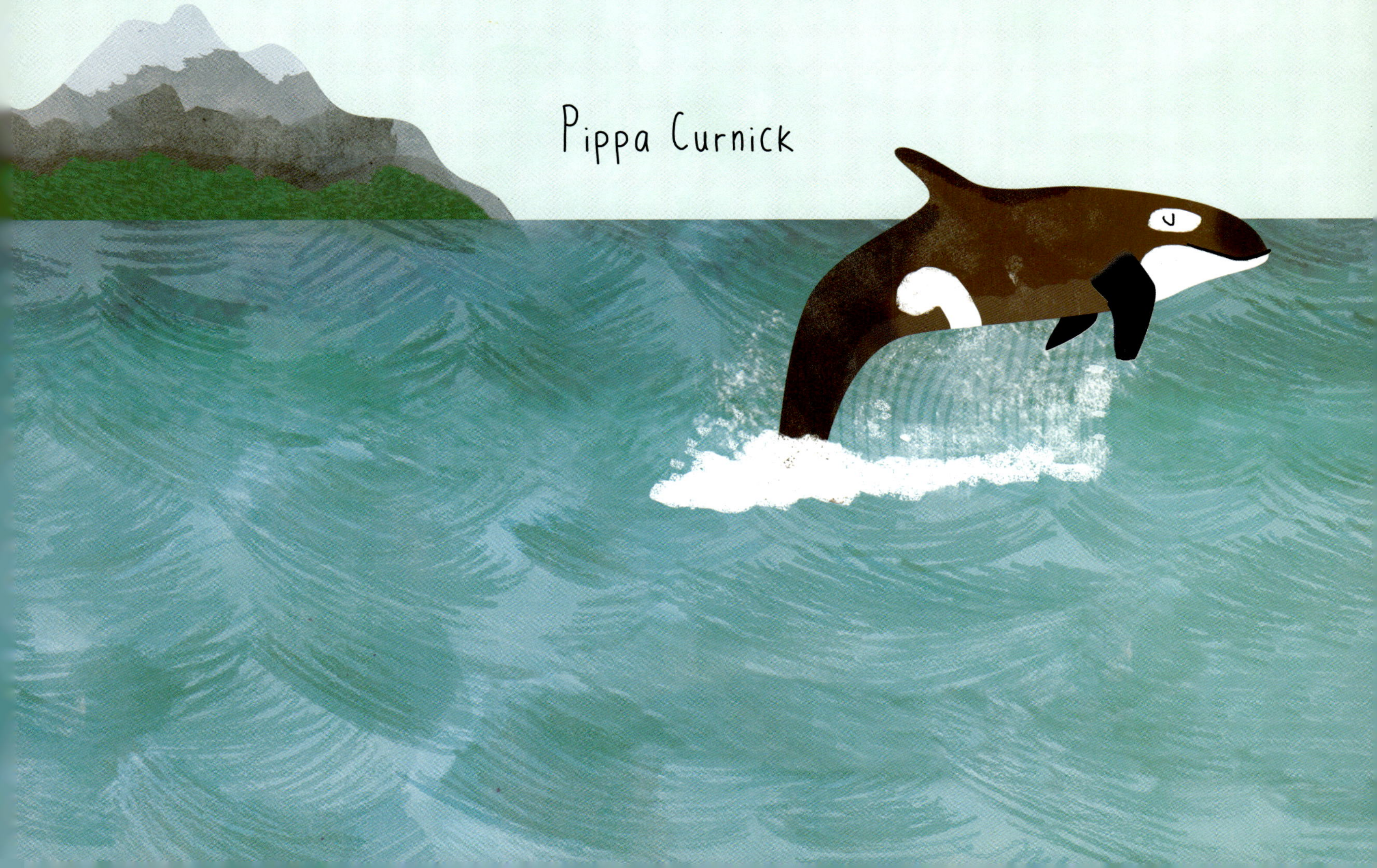

Are you ready for an adventure?
Two explorers, Marco and Amelia, are off on a round-the-world diving trip, and they've invited you to come too!

The best explorers need to be ready for anything. Look at the list below and add stickers to the next page to get ready to go. Cross the items off the list when you've stuck them on.

Ocean Explorers' Kit

MARCO
* Wetsuit
* Snorkel
* Mask
* Flippers
* Towel

AMELIA
* Wetsuit
* Snorkel
* Mask
* Flippers
* Waterproof Camera

Rockpools are teeming with life. From crabs and limpets, to starfish and seaweed. Use your felt-tip pens to make this rockpool lively and bright.

Marco, Amelia and their friends are looking forward to a day of swimming, but their flippers have sunk to the bottom of the sea! Can you figure out which flippers belong to which diver?

1.

2.

3.

4.

A.

B.

C.

D.

The Great Barrier Reef in Australia is so big it can even be seen from space! There are over 1,000 species of bright fish and cool coral to be found here. Use your stickers to complete the reef.

Experts think that there are a whopping three million sunken ships at the bottom of the world's oceans. Help Marco and Amelia to explore this one, and find the items listed on the next page.

Sunken treasure:

* A pearl necklace
* Five gold coins
* A silver candlestick
* Two china teacups
* A silver spoon

The deepest part of all the world's oceans is called the Marianas Trench. There's no sunlight down here, and the deep ocean is home to some truly weird and wonderful creatures...

The barreleye fish has a totally transparent head!

The Dumbo octopus floats above the sea floor and can swallow its prey whole. Gulp!

The spooky-looking goblin shark can extend its jaw to catch its food.

This anglerfish has a light on its head that it uses to attract other fish, before snapping them up in its huge jaws.

The viperfish's teeth are so big that they don't fit in its mouth!

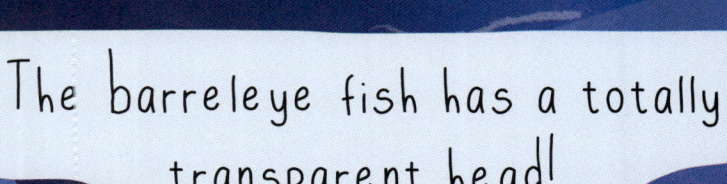

Use your pens to design your own creatures of the deep.

Octopuses have some of the best camouflage skills in all of nature. This means they can change their appearance to blend in with their surroundings, and turn invisible! Use the octopus stickers and hide as many as you can in this scene.

Marco and Amelia are diving in the warm waters of the Red Sea. There's a cheeky little clownfish hiding somewhere. Can you help them to find it?

Eeek! Daredevil Amelia is trying a cage dive in South Africa. This is one of the best places in the world to get up close with great white sharks. Great whites have up to 300 teeth in their mouths and love to snack on fish and seals. Use your stickers to add more scary sharks.

Marco and Amelia have dived down under the ice of the Antarctic, and the water is freezing cold. The animals that live here may have to swim a long way to find food. Use your stickers to add more playful penguins and seals. Brrr!

1. If one of my arms gets chopped off, I can regrow it.

A.

2. In my species, it's not the mother who gives birth to the babies, it's the dad!

3. I can shoot black ink to confuse my predators and help me to swim away.

C.

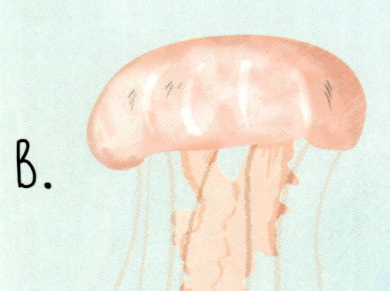

B.

4. I'm the fastest fish in the sea! My top speed is 110km/h (70mph)

D.

5. If I'm attacked, I can make sticky goo come out of my body to cover my attacker in slime.

6. I talk to my family and friends by singing to them.

E.

F.

7. I can make a little light on my head glow to bring tasty fish close to me.

8. I have poisonous tentacles that stun my prey by stinging them.

G.

H.

These slimy sea slugs, sea stars and sea cucumbers make their home on the sandy seabed. They're often neon-bright, to warn other creatures that they are not tasty to eat.

Use your stickers to cover the sea floor in
more eye-catching creatures.

Amelia has spotted the sea creature she likes best out on today's dive — the seahorse! She loves its curly tail. Follow the instructions below to draw one of your own.

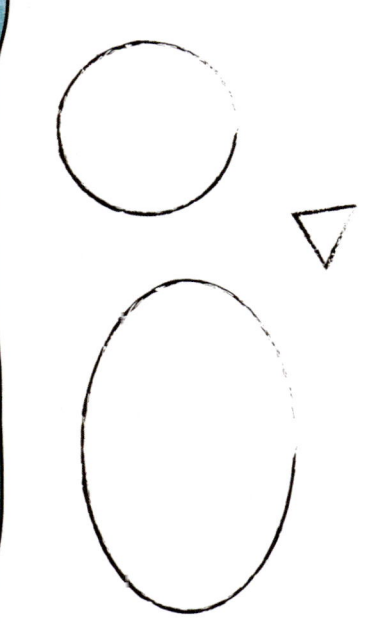

With a pencil, draw a circle for the head, an oval for the body and a small triangle for the nose.

1

Connect the head and the body with a sausage shape, add two lines to finish the nose and draw a fish hook shape to start the tail.

2

Add a frill around the back of your seahorse's head, and a fin on its back. Widen the tail shape and join it up with the rest of the body.

3

Draw around the seahorse in pen and add some stripy detail to its body. Add an eye, then erase the pencil lines.

4

Amelia has started to draw another seahorse here.
Can you help her to finish it off?

Ouch! Join the dots to find out which snappy sea
creature has Marco by the toe!

Start

These jellyfish might look pretty, but their tentacles have a nasty sting. A group of jellyfish is called a bloom. Can you spot two identical jellies in this bloom?

Marco and Amelia have come up for air on a beach in Costa Rica, where a sea turtle's eggs are ready to hatch. Can you help the baby turtles find their way across the beach and into the waves?

Start

Our explorers are visiting an amazing underwater sculpture park in Grenada. It's full of incredible, lifelike statues that are slowly getting covered in coral and other undersea creatures. Wow!

Use your felt—tip pens to design
your own underwater sculpture.

Dolphins are some of the cleverest creatures in the whole of the animal kingdom. They communicate with each other using clicks, squeaks and whistles. Bottlenose dolphins travel in groups called pods and can often be seen leaping out of the water.

Use your stickers to fill the sea with jumping, diving dolphins.

It's time for a trip on a glass–bottomed boat. Can you spot eight differences between these two pictures?

These green spindly algae are called kelp and they grow in large underwater forests.

They're home to lots of types of fish, which are an important source of food for otters, sealions and diving birds. What else is in this kelp forest? Use your stickers to finish the scene.

When lots of fish of the same type swim together, it is known as shoaling. Moving together in a large group like this can help to protect them from predators and make finding food easier. How many fish are in this shoal? Finish them off with your pens.

Off the coast of Alaska, Marco and Amelia are whale watching. In these waters, they can see humpback whales, black—and—white orcas and smaller minke whales. How many of each can you spot?

Up on the surface, everything is calm. But what's going on beneath the waves? Add stickers to complete the scene.

Can you find these items from your diving adventure hidden in the grid below?

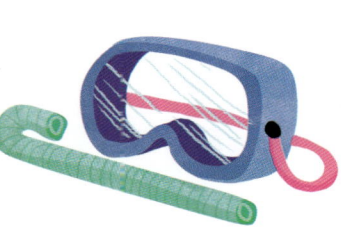

OCTOPUS

SHARK

CORAL

BOAT

SNORKEL

STARFISH

```
W O B L E F X W A L L B
P N K E T S H C O R A L
H K R A H S W R T O P S
D A R F A L P A J E N O
O I L A L J T B V U N C
L S H O T R A N O M 1 T
P U T T U K O C Y 1 H O
R H U C R W B A L O P P
X B R P O E C 1 Q Z L U
C S T A R F I S H J O S
N E L C H S 1 F W O D N
A L E K R O N S X R T A
```

DOLPHIN

TURTLE

CRAB

Marco and Amelia have had an amazing time on their diving trip, but now it's time to head back to dry land and explore somewhere new. Will you join them on their next adventure?

Answers

Check all your answers here... but no cheating!

Flipper Fun

1. B   3. C
2. D   4. A

Sunken Treasure

Hunt The Clownfish

Superpowers

1. D   5. F
2. G   6. H
3. A   7. C
4. E   8. B

Dot To Dot

It's a crab!

Matching Jellies

Turtle Maze

Spot The Difference

In The School

66 fish

Whale Watching

5 x humpback whales

2 x black-and-white orcas

4 x smaller minke whales

Word Search

Stickers to dress up Marco and Amelia

Stickers for the Great Barrier Reef